SALES 101

With Words
All Can
Understand

Written by ,
M. Jason McDermott 75'
Made public 2018

I'D LIKE TO DEDICATE TO AN INDIVIDUAL THAT'S VERY IMPORTANT TO ME.
A PERSON THAT LOOKS BEYOND THE SURFACE , JUST CRAZY ENOUGH TO PULL AWAY FROM THE PACK OF JACKALS AND
EXTEND HER HAND TO HELP RESURRECT A LEFT FOR DEAD WARRIOR LIKE ME .
THANK YOU D.S~F. AND NOW I'M GONNA TELL YOU ALL
ABOUT

THIS FRIEND OF MINE

I think we all need to take some time from our busy schedules . Your busy lives and remember those , whom stood and still stand by our sides today . You know , The no questions asked , still talk to you even when you feel your at your worst , kinda friends . See not to long ago I had a relapse . I mean of course right ? Things were going good again , money was flowing again , no matter what , I could do nothing but win AGAIN . That's when I started partying again , thinking I was bigger than life again , even smarter then the world again , living that fast life of pretend again .
Then , Just as all those old casino's in Vegas , I fell even harder just trying to get back to the surface AGAIN . Next , I move to this little town named Glendale and of course I'm my normal charming , people meeting, pleasing , Libra kinda self. As I continued facilitating that evening's cast of characters and numbing my loneliness through this fantasyland I created for myself. I stumbled across a person that in the end was just like me at my peaks . Someone that had hope , belief in the good of humanity and rarely put herself first. One of those individuals that helps to lift you up , to root you on .
That's tells you to get the fuck up , but in a way that you still know she's your biggest fan . The kind that when the yelling and the knives come out , even though she might be way in over her head , there's no budging her cause , cuz if you're going in then she's going in too . You see I'm not used to that , I'm always the one people goto for the pick me ups , the dusting off , the motivation rather their inspiration when they have none left . However when the shoe was reversed , I'd have those same people give me a little b.s. two line sentence , then roll their eyes as they walked away . See at my fall , my time for truth , there was No ONE there, but this Friend that I've known for now a little over 3 years . The type of friend that even when you're arguing she's still gonna makes sure you have food cause she knows your too proud or too stupid to ask for help . A friend that you can call anytime day or night without them saying wtf as they send you straight to their voicemail . The type of friend that knows something's not right even before you speak . Dolly , I know we've had our misunderstandings and we both can be stubborn ass mules at times , but THANK YOU . Thank you , for being my friend when Ineeded one the most. See that's what separates you from the others and that's what makes you important to Me .

Luv Always M.Jason McDermott

SALES 101

The *ART* of becoming a *GREAT*
Salesperson begins once you've spoken that *2nd* and *6th* word.

ART:

Your Craft . Your Specialty. The Talent which separates you from any Johnny come lately . Your gift or rather the clay you were given once born that you've now turned into an unbelievably breathtaking masterpiece. Your Characteristics , your Skills , your Flawless Knowledge . Your Being , your Essence. The Brain, the Look , your Drive , being Bless'd with an Ambition which non other compares or can even entertain taking from You. This is what You Will be known for .

GREAT:

In sales , in my mind , there is no such word as "Great" .
No , Thank you. You see great is for everyone standing in line. I don't stand in line , the line stands for me . You know why ?

Because I am the BEST.

Trust me when I tell you that everyone comes and will wait to see the best . To hear even a sentence from the best , desperately hoping that some of that Gold which exudes from this larger than life enigma will somehow drip onto them as you walk by .
I understand that sounds extremely arrogant however you're building your best character . The one that wrote the answers to all of their questions.
Assuring them that when the shit hits the fan , and trust and believe it will , that all they need do is call . You see they know , if your voice is calm and relaxed , they've zero to worry about , your in control and Yes , everything is going to be all right. Once again their day can continue as if nothing has happened because your there , and you know everything . More over how lucky are they that they've appointed you their Captain in charge. You see , people always want what they can't have , they usually only want what other people want. They love to talk about themselves and live to be the one , that got what their "step-above person ," was unable to get. They also want to boast and brag all about YOU, the godsend whom was able to make this impossibility a reality . In turn the referrals will now make hunting for listeners a thing of the past as due to your actions they can't stop

boasting rather bragging about you. Now , would you like to know why? It's their pride and ego , their celebratory pat on the back because of course they were the ones to find you. It's because they now feel one up , more complete then anyone in their valued circle. It's because they have you and you my dear friend, You are the best . Welcome to your New World, a world were you are the King.

Were the story pours out of your mouth and the thirsty and starving, with Great appreciation , will eat and drink whatever you're willing to offer them.

Were the client feels they need you more the you need them and are willing to show and prove to you their extreme appreciation , their loyalty for allowing them the ability to participate in

Your vision , in Your drive.

See you've free'd them , you've with a few words , have made them once again alive. They now begin questioning and wanting to forget a life prior to your involvement , rather your entrance. You've earned their trust and now Your words have become their grail. Your opinion determines their internal self value.

They trust in you completely and understand that you have not been sent to hurt them , no absolutely not , you've been sent to do nothing but provide the answers they've been seeking.

Now most importantly Mr. Superstar, never loose track, as most superior Salesman do once in positions of power and trust, is That you NEVER think of your own gains first. Your wants will come, our gifts will come. All thanks to Sale's unspoken Oath. Our selfless Oath to the Sales Gods. To do nothing, nothing but help. Help in every sense of the word because that's what they felt they were lacking, your value was what they felt they needed. This is why they chose you. I mean How could I have possibly been instilled, actually entrusted with such an unbelievably vast surplus of Knowledge, Communication and Understanding? It's Because I'm the best

I am

the Master Salesman

Welcome to my World

TABLE OF CONTENTS

CHAPTER 1. I AM

CHAPTER 2. THIS IS ME

CHAPTER 3. I KNOW IT ALL

CHAPTER 4. UNDER PROMISE AND OVER DELIVER

CHAPTER 5. THE DANCE

CHAPTER 6. IT'S NOT A RACE IT'S A MARATHON

CHAPTER 1. I AM

Do you ever wonder what separates a shoe salesman from lets say a stock broker ? The answer is more zeros.

More zeros at the end of that comma. Sales is a form of convincing . Convincing your audience (customer / client) that they can believe in you. That you are the Most Knowledgable , the Most Experienced , basically their God in regards to this particular subject.
So much so that they're willing to part with whatever it is you're trying to receive. In most cases that's MONEY .
For me , sales started when I was young , lets say my single digits of Life. Your formidable years or for me it seemed more like my survival period.
Now its Time for us to think outside the box . When I say sales, I don't just mean , "hey there X,Y and Z , would you like to
Buy a pack of gum from me ?
It's only 50 cents for 1 pack or 75 cents for 2 ? How many can you handle?" See that's nice , that's basic. However as you evolve you'll realize that you've been a salesperson practically your entire life here on Earth. Sales go far deeper than you may think. From the Time we're born we're constantly selling.

(Example 1)

Let's say as a child , you grew up with a brother or sister in a single parent home. Well , you're constantly going to be fighting or selling your cuteness , your charm , your authenticity to your parent in order to receive more or in greedy situations all of that parent's attention.

(Example 2)

In school , (which usually starts at 5 years of age) you're trying to listen , comprehend and then express your knowledge
Of basically what you just learned. You're selling that teacher the notion that, You do understand what was taught and are deserving of the best possible reward he or she can offer. In this instance it would be the instructors opinion , they're grading , preferably an A.

(Example 3)

When you went to obtain a drivers license you were selling the instructor the idea that you knew how to operate and control a motorized vehicle. That you also would not violate any of the driving laws if that instructor was persuaded enough as to grant you the privilege rather the ability to drive.

(Example 4)

When you meet people for the first time. Or when dating prior to having sex. You're subconsciously selling . Pay attention when you're talking . Who is that speaking ? Is that you ? Kind of ?

Your basically putting your best foot forward and selling yourself to that person . You may say no , but think about it . You've got your nicest or what you believe to be your nicest clothes on. You smell great , hair , teeth , car. You're essentially putting yourself and what you value on display so that person will want to buy it . You're looking to sell them on taking you home , undressing you and then playing with their brand new present .

YOU !!!!
****NOW PLEASE**PAY ATTENTION**AND NEVER FORGET****

Always stay as real as possible. Remember you can get away with a lot in sales , however proper selling does take large amounts of energy. You're only going to be able to fake it for just so long. Eventually your energy , patience and time will run out .

That's when your mind convinces itself that the gains you've been receiving from your effort expelled is no longer worth the value of that effort. The goal here is to always set your sites high.

Determine your actual value , then visualize the level you'd like to achieve . Lastly plan your steps through four mini-goals all designed for assisting you in achieving that outcome . Then stay focused until your goal has been conquered.

CHAPTER 2. THIS IS ME

I hate to say it but the best way to become the smooth , coercive , master of all personalities or better yet the closer, is to present the total package .

I never want to admit this but people judge. They judge you from the minute you walk in the room, from the minute they see an advertisement , from the moment that phone rings. As soon as they see you or hear you , that image or persona begins to build in their mind. This is extremely important to understand if you are that salesman because once that storyline has been cast , it's nearly impossible to reverse the pattern in which their mind travels.

In our world at least as of now there's a competition between people to obtain things that are out of their reach , not what they know they should afford or that's on their level , but rather to have what everyone else is dreaming of. People want to take pride in showing of that shiny new ring, that awesome new vehicle , their super sexy new date. This is all to satisfy ones ego, ones feeling of less than. Cause how could there possibly be any problems when everyone tells them how nice their ring is or how they wish they could have a car like that or wow your date is so fantastic she is smoking hot . You see , we buy things to fill voids within ourselves, and who am I to deny that person of what they , without truly understanding , feel they need.

Possibly the biggest characteristic in becoming a master closer vs a great salesman is :

1. You need to dress for your role.

****Details , Details and more Details***

Redefine yourself and all things involved. This now becomes your new reality and the Star better look Successful. When I first started as a financial advisor I had a few suits (now keep in mind when I say suits , I'm talking about some hand me downs from my Uncle , who was actually only a few years older than me, so yes , he did have a nice eye).

Since I'm giving praise I should also say that until I was ordered to reside with my Grandparents at the age of 13, I had no idea how to dress and felt as uncomfortable as a fish out of water wearing anything but a t-shirt and jeans or a t-shirt and shorts. Black shoes ? Black socks ? Yeah right , I don't think so. Obviously , I realized fast during my first office job the importance of knowing the significance of what they were trying to teach me.

After getting my feet wet in collections , I then passed my series 7 securities (stocks & bonds) exam and it was now about to be my turn. I always was a fast learner and it didn't take long for people to say wow J , you're so shiny , so flashy. I mean come on now , I felt like a million bucks and I'm at the prime of my life. Thinking I am the man in my business management sales career. Rather as I later referred to it as , my high dollar commission , pure cut throat , shark type , swing MY BIG dick of a world. I was on cloud nine until one day I offered to pay one of the more senior broker's (more experienced) lunch tab. It was a $10 lunch place and I figure it would be a cheap way for me to break the ice and get this powerhouse to notice or like me. So I offered to pay the bill and I'll never forget him saying to me , "I'm wearing a ten thousand dollar suit , I drive a brand new Bentley , I made 500k last year and on my way to 750k this year , does it look like I need you to do a fucking thing for me?" Those words even to this day , which is now twenty years later , I will never forget.

So now what was it that I learned from this ? The obvious , not to be an arrogant jerk to someone who obviously doesn't have the experience or even the awareness of how viscous of a game he's placed himself in ? No , I learned that when you start to succeed , it's your obligation to your craft , to the actual spokesman of your business ,You, to invest in the stereotypical material of that industries perception of supreme Success . Hence the flashy , "IT" name brand suit . The mouth dropping Maserati and Mr. ShitHead , if that's not enough for you , well here's my ATM receipt. You see in commission only sales you need to feel that You are that guy and here's my income to let you know that you are no were close to my level pal. Actually here's a tip , once you've saved some money , probably by the next 20 years , well kiddo then come see me.

2. You need to establish a wow vehicle , or something considered the top of the line in regard to the type of industry for which your in. eye catching , not boring . As if validating the persona they feel in that industry is the optima of success. Solidifying their possible doubts.

3. You need to be personable , honest and compassionate in the role you're establishing. find out their fears , their goals , become their phycologist , never stop questioning and establishing their desires cause this will help continual growth of your relationship . This isn't a me or an I type of love affair. You're establishing unity , a partnership , an "Us" capacity. It's not about the money , we don't even need to discuss that any longer . You see , it's about them and protecting as well as understanding what they consider the only thing which holds them together.

4. You better be knowledgeable about your products , your industry , as if you were one of the founding fathers . Never lie or fall into a trap that has been set to see you lie, if you don't know an answer you better learn fast and you better retain it so you never come across as a rookie again.

5. You better have thick skin and not be afraid . People want to direct , deflect or place blame on someone else . Remember they don't make mistakes their perfect. That's why you get paid what you do. Own it , Take it and then Establish control… They need You, you're the best, you're the expert. You can always turn lemons into lemonade.

6. You better master the art of following up , mold them , keep the expectations slightly below what you anticipate . Under promise so you

can over deliver. You work on your terms , don't agree too or confirm something just to neutralize a situation.
They will always remember that one for instance and when you least expect it or are ill-prepared , well guess what that's when they will remind you.
7. It's NOW time to reflect . Look in the mirror and say your name with pride . Realize your value your worth , embrace the trust , the power you have with just a simple word. However never forget there is a thinLine between love and hate and in just one wrong step, one breach of their confidence they will replace you as if they never knew you .Poof , just like that . Remember the expression you're only as-good as your last trade (sale). So , never gloat or stay high for too long cause things can go sour just like that , stay humble .

CHAPTER 3. I KNOW IT ALL

This is the part that separates most from their max potential. Something so simple that I'd say 75% of salesman continuously forget about and that's FOLLOW UP. Listen you could be the greatest master of your craft however if you get a commitment (especially if there's a major purchase pending) you better go get that money. In certain professions you , well actually the Company , since you are usually acting as an agent for that Company , operating in a fiduciary capacity , will be liable for any and all negative market fluctuation. You absolutely DO NOT want to pay for someone else's Gambling loss's. I've seen it when I was a brand new financial advisor cold calling from Rookie Row . One of my fellow rookies accidentally pushed sell instead of buy .
OUCH. That was almost a career ender for my young friend.
Not only did he have to pay for the loss once he realized it 3 days later but then he had to rebuy the stock at the same price it was three days prior to it going up.
All together he was out $25,000. He was lucky enough to catch a break , I mean he did come from a wealthy family , but it could've easily had happened to me and that would've been the end of my career before it even started.
So take your time and *FOLLOW UP , FOLLOW UP*
and in case you forgot ,most importantly *FOLLOW UP.*
Next , Please never take for granted the simple however very obvious fact that :
Success is very powerful , it allows freedom, it allows the true you to find itself. It can breed confidence even a slight arrogance at times. I mean to stay consistent , to stay strong you definatly need to exude an air about yourself , as if life's financial blue print is right in front of you and you've been blessed with the only copy.
However

NEVER let yourself actually believe your own bullshit, never loose track that there are certain things that truly are out of your control.

No matter how many home runs you hit or how cool you think you are remember your only as good as your last sale .
The sad part is that usually once you believe you're the next coming of Jesus Christ , well that's when the slump comes and if you've been bragging , rather gloating over the Financial Guru you've become , well ,   I'm sorry to say that your gonna fall hard . Your ego which was falsely made to begin with is about to go for a possible tragic free fall. If not controlled and corrected , your entire personality could change to the most negative imploding version of yourself. Always stay as humble as possible .
Never forget were you came from. Never forget the true , reason you fight for success , were your drive your passion manifested itself from. The real reason you except nothing but becoming the absolute best. That will pull you out when you need to get back on that bicycle, time for another round.

CHAPTER 4. UNDER PROMISE AND OVER DELIVER

1. This is a biggie…I've come to realize the psychology of sales, is that people (investors, clients, etc.) Will hold you to what you've told them. Due to that, be very careful what it is you promise to achieve in securing that sale because my dear friend you will need to deliver what you promised. The best way to fix this is under promise and over deliver.
2. Here's a prime example. As a financial advisor, when I would sell securities (investments), I knew about 90% of the time, what was going to happen to the dollar value of that investment once the symbol hit the market. Lets not forget, if the price to the client is $100 and my commission is 5%, well it's not rocket science, their investment is going to be priced at $99.5. So if you hard sell on the fact that it's gonna go up initially jumping out the gates. That there's "absolutely no doubt about it, put the house on red, I feel this one". Well, sure they will, they believe in you and you might get them to bite now, but good luck on a future buy. Plus you've just shot your credibility and that client has now lost all confidence in your recommendations from here on out. Total Disaster. That's what happens when you over promise and under deliver.
3. Now if what you were quoting the prospect had a potential return of lets say 8%, what I would do is first establish the price to buy and the fact that your commissions are built into the initial cost. This way when they open their accounts on line they don't have a heart attack when they see the price goes from $100 to $99.50)
4. First step is explain the negative, which fee's or commissions are not negative. Your entitled to make a commission. Next instead of quoting an 8% yield, I would sell a 7% yield.
5. Two reasons, first when or if they complain about the spread in pricing you can advise them of the increase in yield.

6. Second reason is if you pitch 8% and it comes in at 7.5% , then they are going to bitch and complain about the extra 1/2% you promised them, were as if you pitched 7% and it came in at 7.5% we'll now you are the one they're trying to have marry their granddaughter .
7. You could've bought the same exact thing for two separate clients, but the one you quoted or pitched under what you knew was actually going to happen , that's the client you under-promised will actually stay with you and the other will be looking for a new broker as if they were cheated , even though they both spent the same and had the exact same outcome.
8. Another example is lets say you have a deadline attached to whatever your involved with. I always say it's going to take longer to complete. That's an easy one , because everyone gets excited when the projects are done ahead of schedule.
9. The last reason that you under promise and over deliver is that if you set their sights or expectations lower than you feel you realistically will obtain, then you'll outperform and will win more then lose in their eyes. Receiving more and getting it faster then expected will always make a client happy.   **AND WHEN THE CLIENTS ARE HAPPY AND EXCITED , EVERYBODY WINS**

CHAPTER 5. THE DANCE

When I chose a product to sell , first I get to know that product like the back of my hand . The pros the cons , its best attributes as well as it's worst . There's nothing you will be able to tell me about my product that I don't already know. Then once I feel almost as one with my item , I'll next use my mind to visualize the type of individual that would benefit most from this never before seen , limited quantity , genuine work of brilliance that I , ever so heavenly , am willing to let you purchase from me today.

Next comes the debate.

I keep my opening fast , short and direct. A powerful icebreaker , introduction and a quick non informative but open questioned close ? "Hello Mr.Jones , my name is XYZ , the reason I called today is I've got bonds paying 6% totally tax free , do you buy bonds?"

Silence....Now , Here comes the dance . Never take this part too serious.

Remember they don't know you and you don't know them. Their mentality , is that you're not going to sell me . Sure they're going to hear everything you've got to say even question everything twice , but No , No. Mr. fast talker , No , you're not going to sell me today. They've worked way to hard for their money . See that's their mind state , that's what subconsciously they're thinking… however what keeps them present and curious is your personality from that opening introduction. Next the key to winning this debate and switching them from their defensive stance of , 'your just a salesman , a telemarketer That guy that's just trying to fast talk me out of my money' .. Is that Person-Ability. Your personality needs to attract them and attract them in a 10-30 second window. Remain respectful while assuming they are just like you . Speak about your girlfriend , your wife , or when my children blah, blah, blah . If that doesn't catch talk about your pets or possibly your parents , anything that most have had to humbly endure throughout some point in their lives. You're trying to find your similarity , your fish-hooking until you finally hear , yeah you know what , me too. Then bingo , time for you to let that person start opening up as you write down , basically document all that makes them tic. Names of their pets , the age of their kids , if their married , their favorite vehicles.

Anything and everything they tell you now that seems of any personalization , you better write down. At this point you've shifted from a salesman , telemarketer to now , you two go way back as if your old friends . Next , be aware of your time spent on the call.

People do love to talk and when they're on a roll it's hard to cut them off, but never forgot your in control of this conversation , it's your dime and now that you've gained control, it's now your sale to loose. You've just documented a good chunk of their inner thinking , with that information you quickly need to envision which of their obstacles your product's value will best suit.

It's now time to begin.

Time to begin the debate ,the why in our little joust . The why you need my product or more importantly why you can no-longer live without my product.

Their motivations they've already explained and if it wasn't for those obstacles currently in their lives now, well we may have never met . To think how lucky are they to have met me. The one that can solve all of their wants. You see I , your best friend now , am the only that knows what can alleviate those issues preventing your perfection. At this point the only thing left to find out is how many of my product you can handle ? That's when you go in for the money . So this is what I have I this is the cost how many shall I get for you ? Then .

SILENCE

I know it's difficult , but be prepared for a for a little hand holding before you get that yes.

Next a Standard response . "Well , I don't really have the money" or "why do I need this again?" or "I don't even know you,"blah , blah , blah . These aren't really questions , you see your now their friend . The sad part is you probably know , just from your quick 30 minute conversation , more about that individual then their actual "real" supposed friends do .

So this questioning is really their way of basically saying , please tell me I can trust you again why
I want this . Ok , tell me one more time , why I need this ?

Now you , Mr. Salesman , will slowly dissolve their objections with actual facts , one or two quick sentences then A brief personalization with one of those pre documented tide bits ,which you wrote down from earlier in the conversation. Throw in your personal thumbs up and end with an open ended close . Something like , "Ok Jim, I definitely think you'll perform that much better and imagine what your wife Becky and the kids ,will think ? Right , its kind of a no-brainer , so how many should we take?"

You see I said ,"We" showing he's not alone , mentally he's now got someone besides himself to blame if things don't go as assumed. I also stated how many should we take as if we better hurry up and take these now because it looks like they're closing up the bag and we aren't gonna be able to get them anymore.

If you know your product your gonna get that person to say , YES . Another major discipline is Once you've heard YES or even OK , after you've asked for the money it's time for you to stop selling .

Stop , Stop , Stop 🛑

The convincing is over , there's no more to gain .
If you keep pitching the only thing your gonna do is talk yourself right out of that sale. I've seen it and done it. Learn from your first mistakes.Good Work . So you've made it through the introduction , you've made it through the debate , you've even secured the Yes .

Next comes the personality .. Revisit their personal information , all you spoke with them about earlier , however now bring some of your own similarities in while asking them what's needed in completing your sale. Keep them entertained , never bored , allow your personality to come in at the end . Then reiterate when all's complete , "Yes , Mr. or Mrs. XYZ , I bought you blah, blah blah, and it's going to your address at blah, blah, blah. I'm so glad I was able to get these for You before they were all gone."

Never forget to say thank you. Don't forget at the end it's always nice to reiterate, "You know, I only have a few of these left , do you happen to know anyone that might like them before they're all gone?" Then ask for the person's name and phone number. Also let them know that your going to say you were referred and ask if it's ok to use their names. Then, real nice like old friends, I say ,"Thank you again and Goodbye" ….   <u>Done and Done…..</u>

Next , do your paper work , don't get distracted. Finish whatever you need to complete your end of this transaction. Then follow up till the money clears. Cha-Ching , You , are the CHAMP.   You'll now be feeling on top of the world . That close , that rush , your gonna feel Great. Yes , sir , your gonna feel like almighty God himself at times and everyone is gonna want to talk to you , to ask you questions , to ask how you did it . Plugged in , just feeding off your energy . That's when you get back on the phone . Don't be mean but it's your time , the best time to sell. Feel that rush , feel your energetic magnetism working and manifest for you. You're no longer thirsty , No , your now selling from the power position , stress free and all those you pitch can feel it too. You don't really care if they want it or not , similar to the girl that likes the guy that ignores her. Stay twice as focused after every sale , STAY ON THE PHONE and if you continue SMILING AND DIALING , you can Watch your sales come pouring in.

Chapter 6. IT'S NOT A RACE IT'S A MARATHON

This is something all good Salesman need to hear. Don't worry or listen to what other sales individuals are throwing at you. For one they're bragging about their sales , how much commissions they've made , basically how they're the biggest , baddest jerk on the mountain and their dick rolls all the way down to the start, so you better use both hands when you climb on. Bottom line is , they are not you and you are not them, they're trying to distract you, trying to fluster you , trying to disregard the one thing that will prevail over all of their self inflated sales tactics and thats your integrity , the magnitude of your Conclusive , All Knowing , Positive Energy. Your C. A. P. E. The way your integrity , your genuine connectivity and relate-ability has allowed you to now project your will onto them. Next they will realize , that since you've said it and were so "matter of fact" about it , that they would be actually embarrassed if it was found out that they refused what you selflessly just presented them. Deal closed. Closer . You will never be questioned or second guessed again. Never , at-least till the next time , will you be labelled as defeated. A defeated salesman is a dead salesman. You need to believe that that next person you speak with is going to be that unbelievable godsend from your dreams. Your home run , your whale , your career define'r. The next one is always the big $ one.I've seen people come out the gates like a rocket-ship and what do they say , what goes up at some point always comes crashes down.   You'll also see the Yo-Yo effect especially if your company keeps monthly sales graphs. Those will be the people that one month their up in everyones face, you know , the overnight superstars. Then reality humbles those self-only , energy suckers over the next month or two and hey , were did they all go ? Chirp , chirp , nothing but crickets. Me, I've always been the kind that aspires to do better this month then last month, to basically be stronger at the end of the fight than I was at the beginning. If you stick to the basic fundamentals , even back to the original scripts- given you , you eventually will get it .

Always remind yourself that this isn't a Race , it's a Marathon. You do plan on hopefully being in business longer than just this month, right? So , don't beat yourself up to hard. but each month figure out what you did wrong and consciously make the Corrections needed. You don't want the same mistakes from last month ever happening again. Lastly the only person you are truly ever competing with, is yourself and the way you envision your desired future based on your stature right now. Nobody else has your bills, your pressures or the demands you've put upon yourself . Remember this expression, "It's not what you make it's what you keep". Try to keep your overhead as low as possible in the beginning. Not to mention try to always stay as positive as humanly possible. Believe in yourself. Believe that if you are true , that divine energy will always guide you to glory.

YOU'VE EARNED THIS . YOU , ABSOLUTELY DESERVE THIS.
Live in the Levels….

Remember , it's never easy to get to the Top and even harder to maintain that Pinnacle, so enjoy the Journey.
SEE YOU THERE**MJM1975**

Thank you for reading my personal insight on building a top-tier , Sales' personality:

SALES 101 - With Words All Can Understand

I'd also like to thank all of those that stood by and didn't bother sheepishlylistening to fake gossip , rumors or others manipulated personal character assassinations against me. Instead many chose to question , WHY. WHY this group would offer such slander and even waste their energy on a nobody like ME ?

What does J know that they're trying to hide ?

WHY are "Power Players" deliberately trying to nullify my existence ? WHY ? WHY? And Really ? WHY?

Thank you for not believing everything your told and once again asking WHY. Here is some Truth that you can bank on tho and that is - My energy will never let you down and I am willing to speak for those whom feel they have no voice.

I believe that with the Power of Positive Thinking mixed with Desire and Truth , Good will always prevail . There's now zer0 reasons anyone needs to settle on scraps when others have

UNUSABLE ABUNDENCES ..

THE DREAM KING

PEOPLE b4 MONEY - EVERYBODY DESERVES 2 DREAM

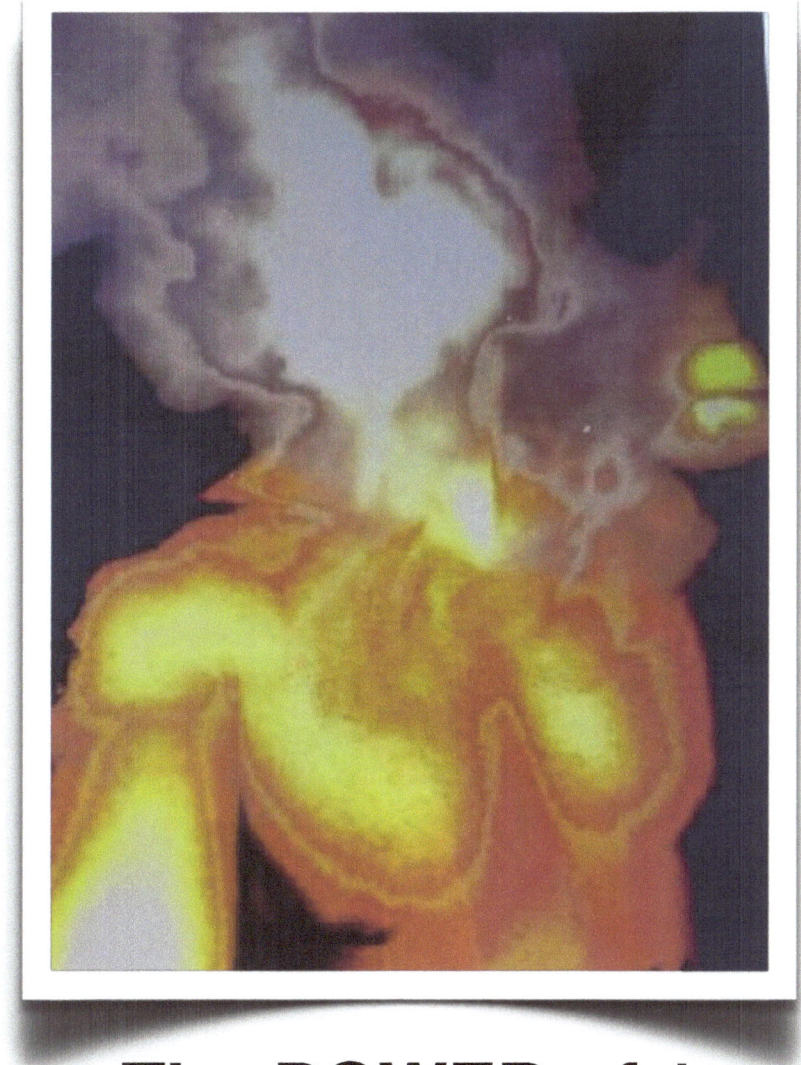

The POWER of 1

All the years of instability , of anxiety
the constant feelings of isolation That
They , were out to get me.

BY M.J.McDERMOTT 75'

The noises, the nightmares, the lack of memory from my first 5 years on Earth. Who is this, this "They" and why doesn't anyone seem to care? Why do they want me to feel alone? Why do they want me to make love to only them, only one. When, even they themselves carry the burden of acting desperate for love from anything or anyone for that matter. I've since come to realize that I don't belong here. These people, this man this woman, they truly have no compassion nor desire for my happiness. No, instead they seem as though they've planned for this exact moment. For the day the innocent, trusting, eight year old boy became closed off and one within himself. However at 12 years old I was no-longer hidden, no-longer isolated. I finally became freed from the shadows, from my seclusion.

But then again came the screams, the nightmares, the burning, the lack of memory from my first 5 years on Earth. Oh, they acted as if they cared, when in reality I was only a bargaining chip, a ransomed commodity, and at the end of the day I was just good for their pockets. I once again was left to question why? Why does it feel as if there is nothing running through my body but confusion? Why do I carry so much of everyone else's sadness and pain?

Then as I grew older and through the fire a lot stronger. I came to realize that the People I once ran too, the people I was distributed too and told I could trust. You know the people we're meant to feel safest with. Those were the beings I should have been fearing, those were the "They". They whom he called his Mom, his Dad, his Grandparents, his

Sisters and at the end , sadly enough even his friends .

    They were the ones that made him feel as if he was unwanted. That he wasn't good enough , that it was all because of him , that their lives as well as their dreams were never achieved . That all was just abandoned , shelved and because of his creative imagination they were sadly left without . AS if this karma , this guilt , this burden was his soul's debt . However after all the lies , after all the positioning , after all their misguided brokered lesson of life . Finally the truth could no longer be masked . That these frauds , these actors were secretly filming all His reactions to their sinister directed situations . Hypocritically and purely for their OWN financial gains . Modern day slavery , trafficking of the worst kind . That I , the burden , was actually the star of all their

own nightmarish fears. Then at the end, when they wanted to all go home and leave the field, it was I, their "enigma" standing strong, soon to be living the life they were all dreaming of. I now empathetically feel sorry and disappointed that their Legacy's foundation arose at the manipulation and total distrust of the only one that actually had UNCONDITIONAL LOVE 4 ALL.

Michael JASON McDermott 75

MAY GOD HAVE MERCY ON YOUR SOULS

www.ingramcontent.com/pod-product-compliance
Lightning Source LLC
Chambersburg PA
CBHW051826210526
45473CB00005B/1752